FIRST THINGS FIRST

When Writing Your Book & Creating Your Legacy!

A Comprehensive Guide to
Write, Publish and Market Your Book.

Karina G. Felix

Published by
Ingenious Publishers Inc.
West Palm Beach, Fl

First Things First
When Writing Your Book & Creating Your Legacy!
A Comprehensive Guide to Write, Publish and Market Your Book
Lifestyle Enhancement, Self-education, Self-Improvement

Copyright © 2021 - Karina G. Felix
www.KarinaGFelix.com
Lifestyle@KarinaGFelix.com

Editor: Lori Robinson
Cover Design: Karina G. Felix

Published by:
Ingenious Publishers Inc.
info@IngeniousPubishers.com

ISBN: 978-1-7329696-3-6   Print
ISBN: 978-1-7329696-4-3   Ebook

Library of Congress Control Number: 2021900488
Printed in the United States of America

    The paper used in this publication meets the minimum requirements of the American National Standards for information Sciences – Permanence of Paper for Printed Library Material.
    All rights reserved. No part of this book may be reproduced or transmitted in any form or by any means, electronic, or mechanical, including photocopy or recording, or by an information storage and retrieval system, without permission in writing by the author. All translations of this work must be approved in writing by the author. Please contact Ingenious Publishers Inc. for permission to translate and distribution agreements.

To order copies for you, your group or send as a gift, go to
www.KarinaGFelix.com

First Edition

Copyright © 2021
All rights retained by author and publisher
All rights reserved

First Things First - Creating Your Legacy

DEDICATION

I dedicate this book to the most
creative person in my life, who
inspired my creativity and influenced
my enjoyment of reading.

My mother
Gladys Peterson Felix

and

the inspiration for my legacy;

My children
Kiara Fedele and Sergio Fedele
Thank you for choosing me.

ACKNOWLEDGMENT

My gratitude and appreciation
goes out to the people that stood
by me throughout my journey.

Thank you to
Ruth Torres for all your theoretical knowledge,
Anna Bourne for staying in the Spectacular Now,
Dawn Fresch for bringing spontaneity back into my life, and my sister
Natasha Felix for choosing to join the Felix clan.

A special acknowledgement to
my editor, college roommate and cheerleader
Lori Robinson

and those too numerous to mention.
You know who you are!

THANK YOU!

TABLE OF CONTENT

First Things First 1
Your Sacred Space 3
Tools 5
Timeframe 7
Writing in Progress 9
Choices, Choices 11
The Content 13
The Flow 15
The Cover 19
The Blurb 21
Working with an Editor 23
The Layout 25
ISBN, Library of Congress 27
Going to Print 29
Partnering with a Publishing 31
Platforms 35
Distribution Channels 37
Book in Hand 39
Marketing & Promotions 41
Testimonials & Reviews 43
Bestseller Lists 45
Royalties 47
Your Legacy 49
Celebrate 51
Check List 53
About the Author 66

"We write to taste life twice,

in the moment

and in retrospect."

--Anaïs Nin

FIRST THINGS FIRST

Publishing a book is more than just writing words, thoughts, and ideas. A book also gives you a sense of accomplishment. The time, effort, and resources it takes to sit still day after day and make this your focused goal until completed is a task of itself, let alone the research, finance, and consistency to reach the end game.

Writing a book is now an even playing game that is available to everyone with a drive and passion for sharing their knowledge, experiences, and best-kept secrets. Many authors are using their writing skills to earn passive income, as a stepping-stone to other opportunities or to leave their legacy behind for their children and family.

Either way, you look at it, writing a book can be gratifying and satisfying all at once. With that said, I would like to encourage you to take a chance and build up that courage to share what you know; the journey you undertook on this earth, accumulating ideas, experiences, wisdom, and stories.

This short comprehensive book-publishing guide will help you navigate the various possibilities available to you in getting your book published. It could be simple and less time-consuming when using a publisher or go it alone and figure it out slowly one step at a time.

There are many resources online that can help you figure out all the steps needed to publish your book. In this guide, I will touch on the programs and sites I've used as a publisher to publish my clients' and personal books.

YOUR SACRED SPACE

Where to start?

Before you begin your writing journey, it is vital to have consistency in the process; therefore, the need for a writing space is essential. Once you dedicate a specific area in your home, office, or whichever place you choose just for writing, your subconscious mind will automatically recognize that it is time to write.

It will go into a focused work-phase because it will remember what you do there. It's part of creating a comfort zone to put you in the right writing frame of mind.

It also makes it easier if you have all your necessary tools readily available to you. Each time you have to go looking for something, you lose your train of thought, which breaks the ebb and flow of your writing.

So, first things first; choose a location that is conducive to inspired writing.

"If you don't have time to read, you don't have the time (or the tools) to write. Simple as that."

--Stephen King

TOOLS

What tools do you need?

Your writing tools are the props you need during your writing cycle. You don't want to be derailed off the train tracks just as your flow starts.

Decide whether you will be writing in a notebook or directly on your laptop or computer. Make sure everything is charged and ready to go.

Have a pen, pencil, and notebook next to your computer, so when new ideas pop up in your mind, which it will definitely do, you can write it down immediately and can look back on it later when you take a break.

If you switch your focus to the new thought that presented itself in your mind immediately, you will lose focus on the idea you were busy writing at the moment. That interruption will slow you down, and it takes time to get back into the flow.

My suggestion is to keep a notebook, or sticky notepads close by, and when these thought surfaces, write it down with a short note with the intention to look into it when you take a break. Make a note of the subject or topic you would like to include or delve deeper into it.

This way, when the assigned writing session is finished, you can go back to the note and work solely on that new idea or topic that appeared in your thoughts as additional information. Then you can find the right place to insert it into the book.

TIMEFRAME

What completion date?

Schedule a daily time slot that you would dedicate just for writing. Pick a time of the day that is conducive to your heightened creativity, quiet, and dedicated time. Every day when you know exactly where you will be and what you will be doing for those specific amounts of hours, this process then makes the flow of writing easier.

It creates anticipation of excitement, knowing that soon you will be sitting before your computer and getting to work on your manuscript. You are fully aware that there is an end result and a work of art that will be created by you and enjoyed by others in the future. The end of the race should be as exciting as the race itself. Do not deprive yourself of enjoying the journey along the way; what I call the scenic route.

Also, give yourself a deadline. We tend to feel that if there is no deadline that there is also no urgency. The issue with this statement is that without an assigned deadline, you may drag the writing out and not give it the attention and dedicated time necessary to get the book written, let alone published.

Break it up in chunks. If you give yourself one month to get the book written, then figure out how much time each day and week you'll need to get it done. Strive for an earlier date, with a backup later date. This gives you a bit of cushion time for any unexpected interruptions or circumstances that may arise during this time. Family, friends, and life in general may get in the way. But it should not be the excuse to stop completely or delay your progress for too long.

Depending on the size of the book, you may schedule a three-month timeframe to give you enough time to write without feeling overwhelmed and still having time for your routine life.

Having a dedicated finishing timeline keeps you on track. It also makes you accountable for reaching an end goal. It is easy to put it off for longer than is necessary and dragging it out for far too long. Hold yourself accountable to an end date.

WRITING IN PROGRESS

Do not disturb.

We believe that we can be productive and focused even with a buzzing phone or notifications going off unexpectedly. We claim that we can sit for two hours and write diligently and won't be distracted even if our phone vibrates softly; that is not accurate.

When you are in the flow of creative writing and your Muses are right there with you writing right alongside you, at that moment, they have your undivided attention, and you are in the zone. A ringing phone, notification ping, or vibrations are enough to distract you if only for a Nano-second. That Nona-second is enough to kick you out of the zone.

You may feel that you can get right back into it, but usually, the whole process slows you down, and you lose your train of thought. Phone notifications create a sense of urgency and anxiety. Even though you tell yourself you will not answer, your subconscious mind is curious to know who, what, where, when.

So, for the sake of your creative Muses appreciation, turn the phone off completely or turn off all notifications and vibrations. Better off, leave it in another room for better results. Also, notify any family members in your household that you will be unavailable for a certain amount of time as you write your book.

Ask them not to interrupt you for anything unless it is a major emergency, or if the house is on fire. Get in a room where no one else will bother you and put a sign up saying, "Do not disturb, Writer at Work!"

CHOICES, CHOICES

What type of book? What Genre?

There are so many different genres out there; fiction, non-fiction, romance, novels, short stories, self-help, transformation, spiritual, and the list go on.

There are categories and subcategories and sub-sub-categories. I know it sounds complicated, but I assure you it takes a few tries before it all makes sense. Everyone has a pain point they want to resolve. What do your readers need to know or would enjoy?

You may have a few different ideas in your mind of messages or stories you would like to share with a broader audience. You might have had an experience you've been through that you believe could help someone navigate their life differently if they knew they were not the only person in such a situation, or you can help them find ways to recover and heal. Your information can have a transformative effect on someone and reach them at just the right time when they are in need of this affirmation.

You may be interested in writing a fiction novel or transform romantic thoughts into a novel. These may be one of your many desires. Either which way, the goal is to decide first off what genre you will be diving into for your book. Search Amazon books for the different categories available in different genres.

This will help pinpoint the direction to take to get the most out of your writing. If you employ a publisher they will assist you through this process and make suggestions to facilitate your clarity and direction.

THE CONTENT

What a great idea!

You know you have a book worthy idea dancing around in your head, but it seems like a massive project to tackle; now what?

What I do to give myself an overall overview of my story idea as well as the direction I want to take is I always start with the chapter's layout. I write a list of the different things I want to discuss in the book, and then I rearrange them according to the sequence I believe it should follow, and then I work on one chapter at a time.

Sometimes, if you are writing an autobiography, semi-biography, or storyline, you can freestyle as much as possible. Once you finish the outline, you can read what you wrote and continue to break it up into smaller segments according to the storyline.

For example, in an autobiography, you may break it down into what prompts you to want to write the book, then a flashback to the beginning, and break it down into your childhood, teenage years, your parents, an unexpected encounter, an aha moment, etc. up until the end of the story.

There could be a consistent life timeframe of the story, or you can have flashbacks to keep the reader engaged and interested.

The first sentence of the book should capture your readers immediately. Engaging your audience right off the bat is of utmost importance. Spend time deciding how you will introduce your book to your readers.

THE FLOW

Let's release the flow.

Once you have created your chapters, it's time to write. I suggest that you write without worrying about typos, sentence structure, and all the rules and regulations that go with the English language, or any language for that matter.

Once you start writing, you want the creative juices flowing. Let your mind and fingers do the work. This will be the first draft of your manuscript.

Only after you feel that you are done for the day, when the free-flowing creative part has slowed, either because you are tired, thirsty, hungry, or just need to get up and move, this is when you'll have a chance to look over what you've typed and may then make any necessary changes and adjustments.

What I've experienced in my writing journey, is that once I've purged all the information I want to get out of my head and onto the page, I take a break and step away from the computer. It could be lunchtime, a walk, a drink of water, whatever you need at the moment to take you away from the project will give you a new perspective when you return to it. This break gives you a chance to clear your thoughts. When you get back to the computer, you'll have a set of fresh eyes when you read over what you've written. This process allows you to make changes, adjustments, and deletions if needed.

At this point, just read through your manuscript slowly with attention to detail. Make sure it makes sense to you and that it would make sense to your readers. Use this practice to fix typos, sentence structures, undeveloped point of view, and other details. Sometimes writing so much and so fast, because the flow is so smooth, we don't fully write out our complete thoughts. At times you may have to elaborate deeper on the topic or issue.

Break down those chapters further into minuscule pieces. Remember, you are telling a story that you know by heart because you lived it or have the knowledge, but it will need a more in-depth explanation for someone not in your shoes to understand it.

Writing is not the same as telling a story verbally. In a verbal conversation, we tend to give just the highlights of the journey. In the book, you have to provide details, descriptions, explanations, background, and deeper insight. You have to take it entirely apart and expose your true feelings and reactions of the moment.

Be humble and vulnerable. It will transpire onto the pages and connect deeper with your readers.

> "Start writing,
> no matter what.
> The water does not flow
> until the faucet is turned on."

— *Louis L'Amour*

THE COVER

Are they judging my cover?

The cover of your book is the first line of connection with your readers. They may say, "Don't judge a book by its cover," but most readers do judge a book by its cover, followed by the description on the back. Your cover is your book. It should tell a story without words.

It should be clear, attractive, and eye-catching. There are several things you must consider with your cover: design, color scheme, font style and size, a catchy title and subtitle, and an engaging description of the book. You will need a graphic designer to create a captivating cover to entice readers to want to pick it up and find out more about it. There are several freelancers and online designers sites you can use to design your cover. Just remember that they may charge a lower fee and therefore produce a lower quality design.

It all depends on what you are going to use your book for in the future. Your publisher may have an in-house designer they trust and use, which will make the process go smoothly.

"There is no greater agony than bearing an untold story inside you."

~ Maya Angelou

THE BLURB

The "What?"

The blurb is the description of the book that is added to the back page or inner flap of a book. It gives a simple overall review of the content. It is your first effort to market and promote the book. This blurb along with an attractive cover and color scheme is the biggest part of a reader choosing your book over another.

The blurb must be enticing and create curiosity to make the reader want to read more. It is just enough information to get the reader hooked into wanting to buy your book.

So, spend enough time writing out a catchy, and engaging description of the content of the book and what the reader will learn or take away at the end.

"And by the way, everything in life is writable about if you have the outgoing guts to do it, and the imagination to improvise. The worst enemy to creativity is self-doubt."

~ Sylvia Plath

WORKING WITH AN EDITOR

"I can do it myself."

Oh no, you can't! In this world of ,"I can do it myself," thanks to Google and YouTube, it is not a good idea to take on this daunting task. I suggest you use an editor as a second set of eyes to go over your manuscript. You can use a friend as well, but if they are not experienced in this field they may not know what to look for. When you read the same thing repeatedly, your mind gets used to it and overlooks obvious mistakes and typos. Only another set of fresh eyes will pick up those mistakes.

A book I published for a client, even after using an editor and two other sets of eyes, the book still had typos that three sets of eyes missed. So don't skip the editing part; it may be your biggest asset. Readers are so much more educated now and will see typos and mistakes, as the author is not being interested enough to give their readers a positive and pleasing experience with their book.

This could be a turn-off and a reason for a reader not to ever purchase another book of yours. Here are a few other steps I take for the editing sequence. First, I let Microsoft Word spell check find as many mistakes and have them corrected immediately.

Next, I upload the file to Grammarly: Free Online Writing Assistant, or the upgraded professional version that gives more details and suggestions. (www.grammarly.com). This software does spell checks and sentence structure correction. But even that program can miss things. Now it's time to find a professional editor to do an overall sweep of your work.

Editors usually have a fee structure in place for the size of the book, how many pages, and the time it takes to edit your work. You could negotiate a flat-fee structure that will work within your budget. This could be an excellent fit for any new writer getting into this game.

Do not skimp on this part. It could be the deciding factor that makes or breaks your book. Go to my website for a list of editors we've used previously. www.IngeniousPublishers.com/Source

THE LAYOUT

A Good Fit!

There are several options for the feel and look of the book. First, you'll have to decide what size you want to print the book. Will it be a softcover or hardcover? Other options are the color of the inside paper. It could be white, off-white, or cream. Are there any illustrations, and would you like it in black and white or color?

The format must give enough empty space on the inside of the center, to facilitate the opening and turning of pages. You'll have to add page numbers, chapter breaks, line spacing, font size, and font style. Binding depends on the thickness of the book.

Format and layout for a print book is different to an eBook, so make sure you are specific as to which format you will be distributing your book. The printing company will have this information available to you before going to print.

"If the book is true, it will find an audience that is meant to read it."

— *Wally Lamb*

ISBN AND LIBRARY OF CONGRESS

Can You Identify It?

ISBN stands for International Standard Book Number. The ISBN is your book identifier. It is a thirteen number sequence that people use to find and allows you to sell your book online and at bookstores. To be considered a published Author your book must be registered and display this number on the cover and inside descriptions.

Each book format must have a different ISBN number, whether it is an eBook, print, or audiobook. The same number cannot be used for each output of the book.

When you register the book with The Library of Congress you are now able to place your books in any and all libraries in the USA. This is an added bonus to sharing and getting additional exposure for your book.

Reminder: You must mail a copy of your physical book to the Library of Congress.

Library of Congress
US Programs, Law, and Literature Division
Cataloging in Publication Program
101 Independence Avenue, S.E.
Washington, DC 20540-4283

"I can shake off everything as I write; my sorrows disappear, my courage is reborn."

— *Anne Frank*

GOING TO PRINT

Time to upload.

Before uploading your file, you'll need to format the pages. The printing company may have software that allows you to do it on your own, or you can purchase your own software to format your book.

There are online websites with cover formatting software, but this does not necessarily mean it will give you the best print output. I suggest going with the printer's software or if you are working with a publisher you won't have to be bothered with these details.

You'll need to include a Dedication page, Acknowledgement page, Content List, Chapters, Copyright description page, and other details for best output.

Decisions you must make about your book before going to print are color of pages, size of the book, font size and style, graphics or illustrations, inside layout, and cover design.

During the upload sequence, you'll need to fill in all the pertinent data such as the author's bio, book description, metadata, special keywords, categories, etc. This process will also be necessary for the eBook format.

PARTNERING WITH A PUBLISHER

Ready to publish your book?

Anyone can publish his or her own book. Unless you write a book just to say you are a published author, then you do not need a publisher. There are two sets of agreements you can make with a publisher. One is to hire a publisher to do all the above-described procedures, which leave you to only do your part, which is the writing. The publisher then takes all the information and goes through the process from formatting all the way to printing. The next option may cost a bit more but may be well worth the investment.

Unless you are not willing to go all out to promote, market, and create buzz around your book, I suggest you use a publisher with an extended agreement. A publisher will already have a set of tools and connections readily available to get your book published and get it seen on different platforms on the net and other venues. A publisher is a way to go if you would like more recognition and a higher revenue income through your book sales and other venues.

A publisher may already have connections with local venues such as bookstores, libraries, expo, etc. that will give you that additional boost probably at a more reasonable rate. A publisher may already have a list of authors it is promoting.

By jumping on this bandwagon, you get the best of an additional promotional boost. You will be able to share in the joint marketing effort through sweepstakes, email blasts, newsletters, social media, and other avenues of distribution.

A publisher will be able to offer ISBNs, and registration into the Library of Congress, which allows your books to be in Libraries throughout the country. A publisher can take you from point A to point Z, effortlessly. Find a publisher that does lots of handholding along the way and allow them to be your cheerleader. There will be much time, money, and resources invested in your success as well as their own.

A publisher may agree to an upfront fee for its services, or they may even offer a back-end agreement where they will collect their fees through royalties of book sales. Many publishers do not want to wait to get paid, and authors may not have the funds upfront. Some publishers will do a half upfront and half back-end agreement.

This option could be the best scenario for both parties because that means the publisher is in the game for the long run. This can be a joint venture that benefits both entities.

"A writer is working when he's staring out of the window."

~ Burton Rascoe

PLATFORMS

Decisions, decisions!

There are several platforms available to have your book published. Ingramspark, Amazon, Lulu, Audible, and the list go on and on. Presently many writers are using two primary platforms, Ingramspark and KDP [eBook in kindle with Amazon].

These two platforms offer the best of both worlds. KDP allows you to upload your eBook and softcover book for free. Ingramspark does charge a small upload and review fee to make sure the layout and any graphics are clear and will print at the highest possible quality.

Ingramspark has a lower cost per print book and adds taxes, handling fees, and shipping. KDP has a higher price per book, but that includes all the printing expenses but excludes shipping. Both platforms are good choices.

What you must consider is the cost of sales, commissions, and royalty structure of each platform. You can dive deeper into researching it or allow your publisher to handle all the details and fine prints. They have done it before, and they know how to navigate each issue and client individually.

DISTRIBUTION CHANNELS

Seeking Exposure?

Once you've written the book, you can distribute it in several formats; hardcover, softcover, EBook, Audiobook, and personally. To maximize your book's earning potential, it is a good idea to have your book available on all of these different platforms for full exposure.

There may be more expenses involved with this, but why are you writing your book in the first place? Do you just want to have the right to say that you authored a book, or are you seriously looking into influencing people with your story? All work takes time, effort, and resources, and some personal and financial investments.

The distribution channel of each platform is extensive, but it needs momentum from the author/publisher to give it that push. Ingramspark distributes all uploaded content to outlets all over the world; this includes Amazon, Barnes & Noble, and Goodreads amongst so many others.

KDP is strictly for Amazon subscribers and members. Here members can download eBooks and purchase softcover books. There are options of an exclusive right that Amazon uses to promote your book further, but this includes 90-day proprietary rights that only Amazon can use, distribute, and promote your book within that time frame.

You will not be able to do any other marketing from your end. Your publisher will advise you accordingly based on the book's genre, title, and category.

KDP also has a first-time author book contest that pays out a handsome cash prize and full exclusive promotion. You can discuss these details with your publisher or you can research it online

BOOK IN HAND

Yeah, it has arrived!

Now you have a copy of your physical book in hand. What do you want to do with it now? What is the next best move to promote your book?

There are several options available for self-promotion at local and national venues that will continue to shed light on your book. You can attend book readings and signing events in your area. You can participate at the national yearly BookCon and Book Expos throughout the country.

You can do book interviews and podcast gigs and so many other options. You can use your book to drive your agenda of the lessons you shared in the book with speaking engagements and tours. You may have the option to promote and sell your book personally through your own online sites.

So many options to choose from. It is possible to become a household name, but it does take time, patience, and persistence.

"Tears are words that need to be written."

--Paulo Coelho

MARKETING & PROMOTIONS

The real work begins.

This is where the real work begins for your book exposure. Without proper Marketing & Promotions, your book will just be another printed manuscript in the market. This is the step where most authors feel overwhelmed and do not continue to pursue the book's promotion.

In this circumstance a publisher may come in handy. A publisher will help you set up your website and work on social media promotions. They can organize giveaways, create buzz around your book, schedule online interviews, photo-op opportunities, and bookings.

They can represent your book at expos and seminars and even help you get speaking gigs if it's part of your agreement package. You must decide why you are writing this book and what you hope to accomplish with it. How much time are you willing to promote and support it? This is a decision you must make and follow through.

Take some time to decide what feels right to you. Do not for a second let this information overwhelm you. It sounds more daunting than it really is. With some hand holding, it is a smooth and easy ride.

TESTIMONIALS & REVIEWS

What are they saying?

Readers are looking for books that others seem to like or have enjoyed. They may want to read a review of someone else's opinion about your book before deciding if they will purchase it.

Having a minimum of 10 reviews at the onset of the book launch, especially during the pre-sale stages, will give your book that extra boost to get on the Amazon bestseller list. You can personally engage family, friends, and colleagues to read your book and leave a review online.

You can also offer a sneak peek preview on your social media platform and ask readers to leave a review and testimonial in exchange for getting a copy of the book or even a pdf file for free.

"A professional writer
is an amateur
who didn't quit."

~ *Richard Bach*

BESTSELLER LIST

How to get there?

Everyone wants to get on a bestsellers list. It may seem like a far stretch, but it is not as tricky now with online book sales as it was in the past.

Getting on a bestsellers list takes a list of processes that will help, such as categories, reviews, clicks, etc.

Your publisher should already have a system in place that can facilitate the search process. You can find much information online to help you navigate this part.

"I only write when I'm inspired, so I see to it that I'm inspired every morning at nine o'clock."

~ Peter De Vries

ROYALTIES

Is the Queen visiting?

Each printing/distribution platform has its own royalty payout structure, depending on which option you choose to use.

Ingramspark charges an upload/review fee for the book cover and the content. It will tie in shipping cost, taxes, and handling fee once you choose how many books you'd like to purchase.

KDP is free to upload, but a higher printing cost per book, and separate shipping. They may keep anywhere from 20% to 80% of the sale price. This trickles down to the publisher, which depending on your agreement, may keep another 20% - 40% of the royalties for its work.

The balance will be paid out to the author. You can negotiate with your publisher on a payment schedule. Some publishers pay monthly, quarterly, half a year, or yearly. Revenue can be anywhere between $1.00 -

$4.00 per book depending on the sale price. It may not look like much, but if book sales are high due to all of the marketing and promotions, then your chances of accumulating a nice monthly passive income will be worthwhile.

Remember that the book is just a stepping-stone to other significant income earning potentials, such as speaking engagements, coaching, online courses, and more.

YOUR LEGACY

Your book is your legacy.

Once it is created, printed, and uploaded to the World Wide Web, it is there for eternity. This book could continue to inspire others for years and years to come. It can be republished repeatedly.

It can create an ongoing source of income for you and your family, and you can pass it along to your children that they may continue to promote it and receive residual income from a one-time project you choose to invest your time in once.

Even though there are many books out there, offering the same topic and issues as you, the potential to reach your niche audience will connect the right person at the right time to make an impact. Not everyone will read the same books but may be seeking the same topics.

The cover of one book that captures someone's attention will not attract the attention of someone else.

Readers may gravitate to your book cover and ease of reading. So there are enough readers out there for everyone.

We are in the age of self-improvement and living a better lifestyle for ourselves and everyone else.

Never give up hope; never think your ideas are not good enough. We are all blessed with this journey on earth and with a story to share. No matter how insignificant you may think it is, there is always someone else having the same issue and looking for connections with others in similar situations. The advent of online contact has made it possible for all of us to find a channel and a group where we fit in.

It's Your Legacy!
Hear me roar.
Your voice, commitment, and dedication to sharing your story are the legacy you leave behind for a better world for all.

LAST, BUT MOST DEFINITELY NOT LEAST.

CELEBRATE!

CELEBRATE!

Give Yourself a Pat on the Back

Writing a book is a daunting experience. It is time-, resource-, finance- consuming. It is a significant accomplishment in your life; therefore, you must always celebrate your achievements to the fullest.

Get together with friends, organize a launch party, and take yourself out for a treat. Buy yourself a gift. Whatever you do, remember to celebrate, give gratitude, and appreciate your effort.

CONGRATULATIONS!

> "I love deadlines.
> I love the whooshing noise
> they make as they go by."

~ Douglas Adams, The Salmon of Doubt

READY TO GET STARTED?

FIRST THINGS FIRST

– Checklist –

YOUR SPACE
- o   Location: Choose a cool, bright, quiet space dedicated to writing.
- o   Desk or table; uncluttered and organized for ease of flow.

TOOLS
- o   Computer
- o   Pen
- o   Notebook
- o   Sticky notes
- o   Glass of water

TIMEFRAME
- o   Set up writing schedule: time, days, hours.
- o   Create a completion date: Decide how much time you need to finish the book and set a date for its completion.
- o   Break your writing up into chunks. If you give

yourself one month to get the book written, then figure out how much time each day and week you'll need to get it done.

DO NOT DISTURB; WRITING IN PROGRESS.
- o Turn off all electronics that will ping, vibrate or ring; phone and computer.
- o Close the door if possible to the space you're in.
- o Notify family members of your temporary unavailability
- o Put a sign on the door that says "Do not disturb" and tell everyone not to bother you during those precious hours.

CHOICES, CHOICES
- o What type of book do you want to write?
- o What Genre?
- o What categories and subcategories?
- o What is the pain point you want to resolve?
- o What is your message?

TIME TO WRITE
- o Write out the ideas you want to share.
- o Create Chapters layout.
- o Rearrange according to sequence of story
- o Spend enough time on the first sentence of the book.
- o Your Introduction note should pull the reader in. Give it much attention.

THE FLOW
- Just write
- First draft overview
- Arrange and rearrange as necessary.
- Elaborate; go deeper into certain issues, topics or chapters.
- Be humble and vulnerable. It will transpire onto the pages and connect deeper with your readers.

THE COVER
- Design a cover
- Choose color scheme
- Choose fonts style and size
- Write a catchy subtitle
- Write a comprehensive description of the story.

EDITING
- Reread your manuscript
- Get a friend or someone else to read and give you feedback.
- Do a spell check in your word program
- Upload to Grammarly for additional spell and sentence check.
- Hire a professional editor

PRINTING
- Size of book
- Color of inside pages

- Graphics, illustrations and designs
- Fonts style and size
- Upload files to the printing house
- Book options: Hard Cover, Soft Cover, EBook, Audiobook

PUBLISHING

- Decide if you will self-publish or hire a publisher.

SELF-PUBLISHING

- Design and create cover and back of the book
- Setup the lay-out of the book
- Sign up for Library of Congress Identification number
- Purchase an ISBN number
- Fill in all the pertinent data such as author's bio, book description, metadata, special keywords, categories, etc.

HIRE A PUBLISHER

- A publisher will do all of the above and more for you.
- A publisher will work one-on-one with you to get the best outcome and results possible.

PRINTING PLATFORMS

- KDP – Amazon kindle eBook and soft cover print only
- INGRAMSPARK – Hard and soft cover and eBook

- o ACX – for audiobooks distributed on ITunes, Amazon and Audible.
- o LULU

DISTRIBUTION CHANNELS

- o Ingramspark: worldwide distribution, including Amazon, Barnes & Noble and Goodreads. (With additional fee, there is an extended distribution channel).
- o KDP: Amazon and Kindle.
- o Lulu: Distribution worldwide with additional cost, higher print per book.
- o Personal: Website, Social Media, Newsletters, Public presentations, etc.

MARKETING & PROMOTIONS

- o Find local podcasters to interview you
- o Visit local small book retailers to carry your book in their store
- o Visit the local library to have copies available.
- o Find book-signing tours to join
- o Participate at book expos.
- o Create your own event to launch your book.

TESTIMONIALS AND REVIEWS

- o Email all your contacts and ask for a reviews
- o Offer a "Sneak Peek" of the book in exchange for an online review
- o Get a minimum of 20 reviews within the first

few weeks to get noticed by Amazon.
- o Offer pre-sale opportunities
- o Start a Facebook, twitter and LinkedIn campaign

ROYALTIES
- o KDP; 70% and 35% royalties depending where it is distributed and retail price of book.
- o Ingramspark: 35% - 55%
- o Depending on what book type.
- o Publisher's percentage varies.

CELEBRATE
- o Get together with friends
- o Organize a launch party
- o Take yourself out for a treat.
- o Buy yourself a gift.
- o Give gratitude
- o Appreciate your effort.

YOUR LEGACY
- o Your book is your legacy.
- o Enjoy it.

CONGRATULATIONS!

You can download this checklist at
www.KarinaGFelix.com

Notes

First Things First - Creating Your Legacy

First Things First - Creating Your Legacy

Books and Magazines published by
Ingenious Publishers

INNER GUIDANCE STUDIO
Guided Writing Prompts WorkBooks.

CREATING YOUR DESIRED LIFESTYLE!

UNRAVEL: Doubts, Uncertainty, Overwhelm.
FIND: Your Path, Your Purpose, Your True Self.

Sign up for additional Series at
www.KarinaGFelix.com

DANZ'N Magazine

All books are available for purchase at
www.KarinaGFelix.com

Publisher
Ingenious Publishers
www.IngeniousPublishers.com

ABOUT THE AUTHOR

Karina G. Felix

Karina G. Felix wears several hats. She has a passion for reading, writing, learning, and education. She is a serial entrepreneur having owned several businesses in various fields.

She is a Metaphysical Science Practitioner, Lifestyle Enhancement & Spiritual Guide, Ordained Metaphysical Minister, Magazine and Book Publisher, Certified Speaker, Published Author, Expert Panelist, 100 Successful Women in Business 2019 Award Recipient, former Miss Aruba, professional dancer, dance studio owner, dance and academic teacher.

Her blog "Living the Conscious Lifestyle" covers articles on Education and The Evolution of Universal Consciousness: Integrating the Evolution of Humanity and Spiritual Consciousness.

Join her INNER GUIDANCE STUDIO - A Guided Writing Prompt Series; Using the Art of Journaling for Self Revelation, Healing and Balance.

Lifestyle@KarinaGFelix.com
www.KarinaGFelix.com

www.ingramcontent.com/pod-product-compliance
Lightning Source LLC
Chambersburg PA
CBHW071319080526
44587CB00018B/3283